⟨ **W9-BEK-816**

DISCARD

My
FUTURE
CAREER

Working in
Film and Television

Margaret McAlpine

GARETH**STEVENS**
GS
PUBLISHING
A World Almanac Education Group Company

Please visit our web site at: **www.garethstevens.com**
For a free color catalog describing Gareth Stevens Publishing's
list of high-quality books and multimedia programs, call
1-800-542-2595 (USA) or 1-800-387-3178 (Canada).
Gareth Stevens Publishing's fax: (414) 332-3567.

Library of Congress Cataloging-in-Publication Data

McAlpine, Margaret.
　　Working in film and television / Margaret McAlpine.
　　　　p. cm. — (My future career)
　　Includes bibliographical references and index.
　　ISBN 0-8368-4237-5 (lib. bdg.)
　　　1.　Motion pictures—Vocational guidance—Juvenile literature.
　　2.　Television broadcasting—Vocational guidance—Juvenile literature.
　　I. Title.
　　PN1995.9.P75M34　　2004
　　791.43'024—dc22　　　　　　　　　　　　2004045224

This edition first published in 2005 by
Gareth Stevens Publishing
A World Almanac Education Group Company
330 West Olive Street, Suite 100
Milwaukee, Wisconsin　53212　USA

This U.S. edition copyright © 2005 by Gareth Stevens, Inc.　Original
edition copyright © 2004 by Hodder Wayland.　First published in 2004
by Hodder Wayland, an imprint of Hodder Children's Books.

Editor: Dorothy L. Gibbs
Inside design: Peta Morey
Cover design: Melissa Valuch

Picture Credits
Corbis:　Peter Aprahamian 10; Paul Barton 49; Annie Griffiths Belt 30; Paul
Bennett/Eye Ubiquitous 27(b); Corbis 4, 11, 13, 21, 36, 38, 42, 44, 48, 54, 57;
Ricky Doyle 55, 56; Kevin Fleming 17; Jason Florio 29; Julian Hirshowitz 39; Robbie
Jack 31; JFPI Studios, Inc. 40; John Henley Photography 15; Jose Luis Pelaez, Inc. 41;
Helen King 43; Bob Krist 53; Pedro Lombardi 6; Maher Photography 23; Buddy
Mays 32; Tom and Dee Ann McCarthy 35; New Sport 20; Dale O'Dell 52; Tim
Page 25; Photex 46; Neal Preston 59(b); Richard Radstone 9; Roger Ressmeyer 14;
Jeffery L. Rotman 51; Ariel Skelley 59(t); Paul A. Soulders 24; Steve Starr 34; Ramin
Talaie 45; Tom Stewart Photography 7, 47; Larry Williams 50; Adam Woolfit 22.
Corbis Japan:　Amana 37(t). **Corbis Saba:**　James Leynse 27(t), 28; Mark Peterson 8;
Tom Stewart 5; Tom Wagner 33. **Corbis Sygma:**　Eric Robert 12, 16; Jean Paul
Lubliner 19(b); Santan Maria Times 19(t). **Getty Images:**　cover.

Gareth Stevens Publishing thanks the following individuals and organizations
for their professional assistance:　John McGivern, actor, comedian, member
of Actors' Equity Association; Kent Aschenbrenner, Director of Engineering,
Journal Broadcast Group; Steven Turinske, Broadcast Director, WTMJ-TV; Raul
Galvan, Director of Program Production, WMVS-TV/WMVT-TV; Art Wilinski,
Shotwell Film; Clay Simchick, Mo42 Special Effects.

Printed in China

1 2 3 4 5 6 7 8 9 08 07 06 05 04

Contents

Words that appear in the text in **bold**
type are defined in the glossary.

Actor

Actors are people who play character roles in various kinds of productions, on stage, in films, or for television or radio.

At one time, a film actor always worked under **contract** for a particular film company, which means that the actor was paid a regular salary and could work only for that company. Today, however, almost all actors are self-employed and **freelance** for many different companies.

Most professional actors have **agents**. An agent's job is to find work for the actors he or she represents and to **negotiate** the terms of the job and the payment rate.

Many children first learn about acting by taking part in school productions.

The "Big Break"

Unknown actors being suddenly discovered or working their way from parts in crowd scenes to fame and fortune happens — but rarely. Research shows that, today, over 80 percent of working actors have had some professional training, either through a college or university theater program or a specialized drama school.

Acting can be a very undependable line of work, and most actors go through periods with no work, which is known politely as "resting." While waiting for the "big break" into acting, many actors struggle to earn a living, working as temporary office help or in other jobs with flexible work schedules so they can take acting jobs when they come along.

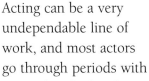

The performance may be called a "play," but the acting is hard work, with lots of memorizing and many hours of **rehearsal**.

To be allowed to perform in professional productions, an actor needs an Equity card, identifying him or her as a member of the Actors' Equity Association, which is a **trade union**. Qualifying for membership is not easy. Most actors must work for fifty weeks with union acting groups and pay a high fee. The unions keep productions from being flooded with nonprofessionals, which forces dedicated professional actors into accepting very low pay.

Main responsibilities of an actor

The performance or the filming is only one part of an actor's job. To begin with, an actor spends a lot of time in **auditions**. First, the actor reads from a script in front of a casting director. Then, if the casting director likes the reading, he or she arranges an audition for that actor with the production's producer and director.

Once an actor has been chosen for a part, he or she needs to give the best performance possible. A good performance involves many, if not all, of the following:

- getting to know the director and everyone else involved in the production
- reading other works by the same author, playwright, or screenwriter
- researching the background of the production (If, for example, the setting of a play or a film is Paris in 1870, the actor needs to find out how the people of Paris lived at that time.)

Doing television commercials is one of the ways an actor can make money.

Good Points and Bad Points

"I love acting. I can't think of any other career I would enjoy more. I've been involved in drama productions since I was eight or nine years old, and there is nothing to equal the way I feel on a stage."

"I feel down, sometimes, especially when I haven't had any real work for weeks, and I'm spending a fortune traveling to auditions."

- memorizing lines and rehearsing them
- developing the character as well as the performance skills needed to play the role

From time to time, all actors, even those who are very well known, take on acting-related jobs such as doing **voice-overs**, filming commercials, recording taped versions of books, or narrating **documentaries**.

Acting work is difficult to find so actors sometimes end up doing more than one job at a time. An actor who has a minor role in a television soap opera, for example, might also be making TV commercials or performing in an evening theatrical production.

Rehearsing can be fun, but it is also an important responsibility.

Main qualifications of an actor

Acting skill
Actors must know how to put themselves into different roles and convince their audiences that they are those characters. They also must be able to affect the audience emotionally, making them feel sad or happy, frightened or relaxed.

Determination
Many actors never gain fame or fortune, and even those who are successful have usually had their share of hard times with no work and little money for living expenses. Actors have to be willing to put their careers ahead of almost everything else in their lives.

Energy
The lives of most actors are far from glamorous. The hours are long and the work, for many, does not pay well. An actor's typical day can involve traveling to auditions; memorizing, taping, or recording; and rehearsing or performing, as well as holding down a nonacting job.

Tech rehearsals can be long and very tiring.

Confidence
To cope with the obstacles and disappointments they are likely to meet, actors need to believe, very strongly, that they have the talent to succeed.

Most young actors need to have at least a part-time job to make enough money to live on.

fact file

Many people start acting at an early age, performing in school plays or at summer camps. Later, they may take evening or week-end acting classes and perform in small theater productions. A professional actor has usually gone on to study at a drama school or has earned a degree in drama or a related field, such as English or communication.

Teamwork

Arguing and tantrums have no place in a production unless they are part of character roles. Everyone involved with the production, onstage or off, is a member of the team, and the team members have to work well together. Also, directors and producers usually try to avoid actors who are known to be difficult to work with.

Multiple talents

Actors who have other talents, such as dancing or singing, may have more job opportunities because they can be considered for more than just acting roles.

A day in the life of an actor

James Fermont

James is twenty-six years old. He finished drama school three years ago.

7:30 a.m. The alarm goes off, and I force myself out of bed. Getting up in the mornings isn't easy because I have an evening job clearing tables in a nightclub. The pay is bad, but the manager is a friend and is willing to give me a flexible work schedule.

8:00 a.m. While I eat breakfast, I read theater magazines to find trade information and audition notices.

8:30 a.m. I travel to an audition for a part in a stage play.

12:00 p.m. The audition is going well, but there's a lot of talent here. I'll just have to wait and see.

3:30 p.m. Back home, I find a phone message from my agent. A television company called her about the audition I did last week for a daytime soap. The series is set in a hospital, and I auditioned for the part of the admission clerk. Apparently, a new role has opened up for a male nurse.

A theater can be a magical place for both actors and audiences.

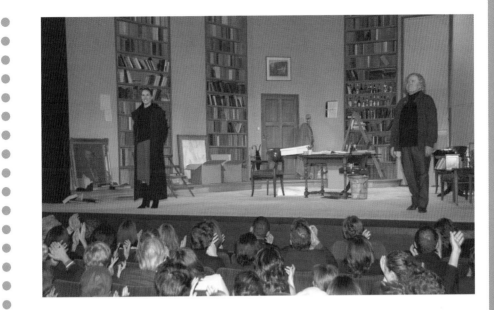

Applause makes the hard work, and the struggle to find it, all worthwhile.

I try not to get too excited, but my agent seems to feel that the role is a strong possibility for me.

4:00 p.m. A friend who runs a small theater group calls to offer me work for the weekend, playing a role in a murder mystery party at a hotel. These parties involve a small group of actors performing a murder **scenario**, then being questioned by the party guests, who have to guess who the murderer is. One of the regular actors has the flu so my friend needs a last-minute replacement. I need the work and accept the job. Every acting job gives me an opportunity to improve my skills.

4:30 p.m. I read through some more theater magazines, then rest for a while before I have to go to my evening job.

8:30 p.m. I'm off to the nightclub for a five-hour **shift**.

Announcer/Program Host

What is an announcer/program host?

Announcers and program hosts are at the front line of television productions, introducing and **hosting** programs. They work for national networks, regional and local stations, and satellite channels. The jobs of announcers and program hosts usually involve one or more of the following:

- introducing programs and giving viewers a brief idea of what to expect
- hosting programs, such as talk shows, children's shows, sports shows, or the news
- **promoting** future programs by talking about them in advance
- broadcasting news bulletins

News **anchors** usually have to write and **edit** the news as well as announce, or broadcast, it.

The wide range of television programs that have announcers or hosts includes news, sports, **current affairs**, cooking, gardening, music, and game shows. Besides explaining what the program is about, the work of an announcer or program host can include introducing and interviewing guests and making sure the program flows well and stays on schedule.

Long and Unusual Hours

Some announcers, especially news anchors, work long hours that can include evenings, weekends, and even time during two or three different **shifts**. Although their basic work weeks might be forty hours, unusual schedules often keep them working longer.

How much of their work is done **live** depends on the job. Often, the work of announcers and program hosts is filmed, or **taped**, in advance. Anchors, however, usually do news broadcasts live. Whether live or on tape, all anchors, announcers, and program hosts work closely with production teams, following detailed instructions and frequently reading from a **teleprompter** or a script.

Many program hosts specialize in particular program **formats**. A prominent journalist may host current affairs programs. Famous entertainers often host talk shows. Well-known chefs host cooking shows. Other hosts may focus on children's programs or reality television.

Making guests feel at ease is an important part of a program host's job.

Main responsibilities of an announcer/program host

One of the most important responsibilities of a program's announcer or host is to keep the program running smoothly. A smooth and successful program depends on good preparation, which may include:

- reading background information about topics and guests
- preparing questions to ask in advance
- scheduling the various parts of the program to fit the show's time frame
- learning the script, if the program has one

When a program does not have a script, the announcer or program host may:

With popular chefs as their hosts, cooking programs can attract millions of viewers.

Good Points and Bad Points

"Working as a television talk show host is a lot of fun. I love meeting people and talking to them about their lives, careers, and hobbies."

"There is a great deal of work to be done before my morning show goes on the air. Hosting a program this early in the day means getting up at about 3:00 a.m."

- read from a teleprompter or cue cards
- decide what to say as the program goes along

When a program is on the air, the responsibilities of an announcer or host include:

- talking to guests and presenters
- delivering information and comments
- listening to instructions from the control room
- watching for signals from the **floor manager**

Children's show hosts have to know exactly what their young viewers enjoy.

Besides performing their responsibilities, announcers and program hosts must have personalities that reflect the styles of their shows. The host of a pop music show should have a bright and lively style. The host of a news or current affairs program needs to be more formal. A children's program host has to be friendly and energetic and able to talk to young viewers as equals.

Main qualifications of an announcer/program host

Confidence
To win the confidence of their audiences, announcers and program hosts must always appear to be confident themselves and in control of their programs.

Communication skills
Announcers and program hosts must have excellent communication skills and clear, pleasant speaking voices so that audiences can easily understand them.

Friendliness
An outgoing personality and a relaxed, friendly manner are very important. Program hosts, in particular, have to be able to make their guests feel comfortable.

Quick thinking
Announcers and program hosts are often faced with unexpected difficulties on the air, but they still have to keep their shows going. They must be able to act quickly, calmly, and tactfully to resolve the difficulties, no matter how sudden or unforeseen they might be.

Part of a talk show host's job is making sure that members of the audience have a chance to speak.

A game show host has to keep the game fun and exciting for both contestants and viewers.

Teamwork

A television program of any kind is the result of the strong teamwork of camera operators, producers, sound technicians, directors, performers, and many others. Announcers and program hosts may be the ones who appear on television screens, but they are only one part of the team.

Technical knowledge

To function effectively as part of a production team, announcers and program hosts have to understand the production process.

fact file

There is no particular path to becoming an announcer or program host. They come from many different backgrounds. Some are specialists in a field such as music or cooking. Others have acting backgrounds. Many news announcers have earned journalism degrees.

Broadcasting is a career in which experience plays a significant role. The experience can come from a college or university degree program or on-the-job training at a local television station.

Anna Costis

Anna Costis hosts a live children's television program. She has a degree in broadcast journalism.

7:30 a.m.   Although my show is on late in the afternoon, I'm already up and having breakfast. There's a lot to be done before we go on the air. My program is aimed at preteens, and it includes news, special features, contests, and interviews with all kinds of interesting people.

9:00 a.m.   I arrive at work and spend some time reading a popular children's book. I'm going to interview the author next week so I need to know what the book is about.

9:30 a.m.   It's time for our weekly production team meeting. Everyone working on the program suggests ideas for future shows, then we talk about the current week's programming.

11:00 a.m.   A celebrity guest I'm supposed to interview today calls to tell me that her plane has been delayed, and she has to cancel the interview.

11:15 a.m.   The production team has an emergency meeting to come up with a replacement for the missing celebrity. We decide to use a short recording of children talking about their views on homework. I have to introduce the piece so I must figure out very quickly what to say.

1:15 p.m.   I read through the material for today's show and review the script. I need to know the order of events and what questions to ask my guests.

2:00 p.m. The guests begin to arrive. I introduce them to the production team and try to help them feel at home. Some of my young guests have never been in a television **studio** before so they need a lot of reassurance.

4:00 p.m. We're on the air.

5:30 p.m. Today's show went smoothly in spite of the last-minute cancellation. Now I have a meeting with the crew about a feature for tomorrow's program.

6:30 p.m. I'm finally on my way home.

All the members of a production team have to work together for a program to succeed.

Program hosts are needed for many different kinds of shows.

Camera Operator

What is a camera operator?

Camera operators film, or **tape**, the action for news programs, feature films, dramas and **documentaries**, commercials, corporate and business videos, and many other kinds of film and television productions.

In recent years, there has been a growing use of video-tape and **digital** cameras for making films and television programs. Many programs are filmed indoors in a **studio**, where a number of cameras may be used, including:

- three to six mounted cameras that can be moved around the floor
- portable cameras that are carried around by camera operators
- cameras mounted on **jibs**, which are used for very high and very low shots

Filming major sports events requires a large camera crew and a lot of equipment.

The Origin of Film

Film started with photographs. The word *photograph* comes from two Greek words — *photos*, which means "light," and *graphein*, which means "to draw." Invented in 1839 by Sir John Herschel, the word describes the method of recording images by the action of light on light-sensitive material.

Pictures from all the different cameras are fed into a **bank** of screens, or monitors, where a person called a technical director picks out the best ones.

Outdoor events, such as the Olympic Games, are either taped or broadcast **live** by outdoor broadcast teams. Mobile control rooms are set up to cover these events. Outdoor broadcast teams often have a large number of camera operators, who use cameras on **tripods** and **mounts** to make sure viewers get to see the most action. While outside teams for major broadcasts can be huge, local teams are often very small, with just one reporter and one camera operator, called a photojournalist.

Without a camera operator to tape the action, local television news reporters would not be able to cover events at the scene.

Many camera operators are self-employed and work on a **freelance** basis. They may be hired to work on a single production or on a series of productions, some of which can continue for weeks, months, or even years.

Main responsibilities of a camera operator

A camera operator's responsibilities start before any actual filming or taping begins. Prefilming tasks include:

- reading the production's script
- planning camera angles and how best to **shoot** the production
- attending **rehearsals** to practice shooting from the planned positions

During filming, a camera operator's main responsibility is to position the camera exactly the right way. Operators wear headsets through which they receive instructions from the production's director and **floor manager**.

Camera operators can't afford to be afraid of heights.

When filming or taping in a studio, the cameras are plugged into electrical outlets with long cables. Trainee operators are responsible for untangling and moving these cables.

Good Points and Bad Points

"Working behind a television camera is exciting and rewarding, but I have had to struggle to become a camera operator. There is a lot of competition for this kind of work. Many of the jobs come through word-of-mouth recommendations so I have to be sure to do my best work at all times. There is also a lot of pressure to keep up to date with all the latest developments in film technology and technique."

Senior camera operators, who, in the film industry, are often called lighting camera operators, have some additional responsibilities, including:

- working closely with the production's director and lighting manager to decide what shots to take
- giving advice on how to achieve certain effects

When camera operators are not filming or taping, they are responsible for making sure that their cameras and equipment are in the right places and ready for use.

Camera work for television is often seen as being less creative and less exciting than film work. One type of television work, however, that can be very exciting but, at the same time, very dangerous, is news camera work. Photojournalists may travel as part of small news teams to remote trouble spots anywhere in the world.

Photojournalists must have many skills. Not only are they responsible for camera work, but they also must be able to do sound, lighting, maintenance, and even film **editing**, when the need arises.

Main qualifications of a camera operator

Technical knowledge

Camera operators must have a great deal of technical knowledge. They have to be able to use many different types of equipment, including cameras, lenses, and filters, and know how to keep their equipment in good working condition. Besides operating cameras, they may also be expected to do other jobs, such as sound recording and film editing.

Confidence

Successful camera operators are able to work confidently in almost any situation, even when faced with difficult or dangerous filming conditions, such as bad weather or noisy, angry crowds.

Artistic skills

Technical accuracy is only part of a camera operator's responsibility. The films he or she shoots must also be good to look at, which calls for some artistic skills.

At a filming site, camera operators often have to take instructions from a lot of different people.

Visual awareness

To do their work well, camera operators need steady hands, good hearing, and excellent eyesight. They especially need good color vision, which means they must be able to see all colors clearly and accurately.

Business skills

Because most camera operators are self-employed and work freelance, they need to have good business skills.

Getting the right shot is not always easy.

They have to be prepared to work in many different places with many different kinds of people and be able to cope with periods of unemployment.

Friendliness

Very often, camera operators and the people they work with have just met, so camera operators have to like meeting new people and be able to make them feel comfortable. They also have to be good team players.

fact file

Many people want to be camera operators, which can make getting into a training program difficult. Successful candidates need to show a strong interest in camera work by having made amateur videos or belonging to a film club.

Camera operators usually need educational qualifications, too, such as college or university degrees in **media** production or broadcasting.

Helen Ashton

Helen is a freelance camera operator who does a lot of taping for cable television programs.

6:30 a.m. Today, I'm working for a small production company that is making a television program about people and their pets. I will spend the day taping a family of pet lovers.

7:00 a.m. I arrive **on location**, which is the family's home, and I talk to the director about the kinds of shots that are needed. I make a few suggestions, then check over my equipment.

7:45 a.m. I set the camera on a dolly so I can wheel it around and take shots from different angles.

8:00 a.m. Some of the taping will be done in the garden. The rest will be done in the house. I talk to the director, again, about the lighting that will be needed indoors.

9:00 a.m. I start taping. Filming animals is not easy so a lot of reshoots have to be done. At one point during the taping, one of the dogs starts barking, which frightens the other animals, and they all disappear.

12:30 p.m. Over a sandwich, I discuss the morning's work with the rest of the production team, and we decide on some new shots.

1:30 p.m. I rearrange the furniture in the living room so I can get some good shots of the family with their reptiles. Fortunately, snakes don't bother me.

4:00 p.m. I load up my equipment and go back to my studio to look at the shots taken today.

6:00 p.m. The day has gone well, but there's still a lot to do. Tomorrow, I'll be taping the family's fish so the day should be more peaceful than today.

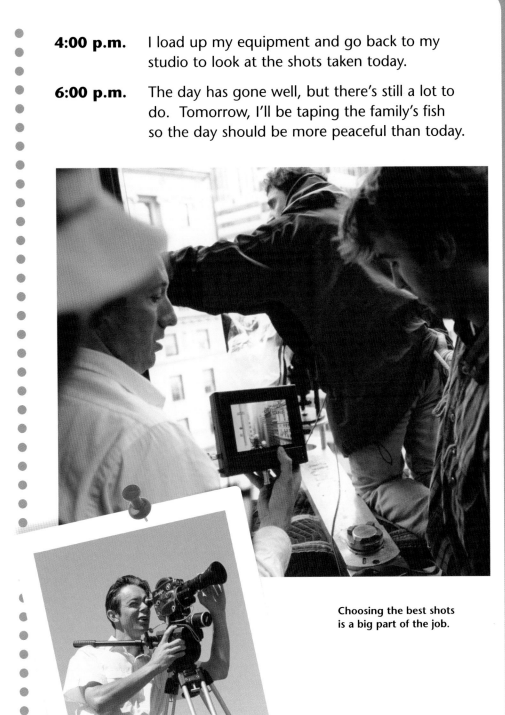

Choosing the best shots is a big part of the job.

Camera equipment is expensive and must be treated with care.

Director

Directors are the people who have creative control over a film, television, radio, or theater production. This control extends to all of the following areas:

- performance
- **sets** and scenery
- lighting
- **props**
- costumes
- makeup

Everyone working in these areas, including actors, set designers, construction workers, lighting and sound engineers, and camera crews, answers to the director. The director tells people what to do and when to do it.

Directors must work closely with a production's technical crews.

Filmmaking History

The 1941 movie *Citizen Kane* is one of the world's most famous films. It is important in the history of filmmaking because it used many techniques for the first time on the screen. These techniques included complicated camera movements and flashbacks to earlier action. *Citizen Kane* was the first film directed by the legendary Orson Welles. At the time, he was only twenty-five years old.

When there are disagreements over how things should be done, the director makes the final decisions.

A director's job involves bringing out the best in everyone.

Most directors work **freelance** and are hired by producers to work on particular projects. The success of a production is mainly the director's responsibility. Whether the project is a simple, low-cost cable program or a huge, blockbuster movie, the director has to make sure that all parts of the production come together with the best possible results.

Although directors are responsible for making all of the final creative decisions, they work closely with their casts and crews, discussing the effects to be achieved and how to achieve them, and they carefully consider the advice and suggestions of actors, designers, technical engineers, and other members of their production teams.

Main responsibilities of a director

A director's first responsibility on a production is to carefully read the script. In some cases, scripts are based on books. The Harry Potter films, for example, were adapted from books written by J. K. Rowling. Other scripts are written just for particular film, television, or theater productions.

As directors read scripts, they form ideas of how they want characters to be played and what the set, lighting, and costumes should look like. The next step is to talk over these ideas with members of the production team, which usually includes people in the cast and crew and sometimes includes the producer. Directors may change their ideas, at times, because of cost or because someone else has a better suggestion.

An assistant director makes sure everyone is ready before the cameras start rolling.

The director is present during all stages of production, including **rehearsals**, filming, and sound recording, to tell the cast and crew what he or she wants.

Good Points and Bad Points

"My last job was as the assistant director of a six-part detective series. The work was very exciting and enjoyable."

"Becoming known as a director in the film or television industry is difficult. You have to be prepared to spend a lot of time running around doing whatever people tell you to do."

Props must be placed on a set in exactly the right positions.

In television and film productions, the director's last job each day is to view the **rushes**, which is the **unedited** film shot that day. If there are problems with the rushes, a **retake** may be scheduled for the following day.

In a big production, such as a feature film, the director usually heads a team of several assistant directors. The first assistant director works closely with the director. Other more senior assistant directors are normally responsible for the following tasks:

- keeping order in the **studio** during filming
- passing on instructions to sound and camera crews
- putting props in the right places
- making sure that the studio is safe to work in

Junior assistant directors are responsible for making sure the production runs smoothly each day, which includes:

- taking care of actors' needs
- making sure everyone comes to rehearsals on time
- checking that actors are in the proper costumes and makeup

Main qualifications of a director

Nobody starts a film or television career as a director. It takes experience, as well as talent, to work up to this very important position. Successful directors have:

Determination
A lot of people want to work in film and television, and finding a job in a field that has so many talented people looking for work is not easy. Anyone who wants to be a director has to be very determined and ready to compete.

Imagination
Directors must be able to visualize how they want a production to look by simply reading the script.

Acting talent
Directors need to know how to act in order to advise and direct other actors. Many directors have theatrical or acting backgrounds.

Technical knowledge
To be able to give instructions to a production's technical crews, directors need to know how cameras, sound systems, and other kinds of production equipment work.

The filming for some productions involves long periods of time on location in places all over the world.

Communication skills
One of a director's most important responsibilities is giving clear instructions, sometimes to large numbers of people, including acting instructions to cast members,

A production's camera crew depends on the director's artistic and leadership skills to know what and when to **shoot**.

fact file

Important qualifications for a film or television director include talent, hard work, determination, and, sometimes, just plain luck. There are no other specific requirements. Some directors have worked as actors, while others have degrees in film- or **media**-related fields.

lighting and sound directions, and requests for changes to sets and props. Directors also must be able to keep a lot of information in their heads.

Leadership skills

Making large groups of people work well together requires a patient, tactful, and, above all, strong leader. A successful production depends mainly on the talent, skills, and leadership of its director.

Sam Birch

Sam is working on his first directing job. He is a junior assistant director on a feature film.

8:00 a.m.   I'm at the studio. This film is being shot both in the studio and on location in several different parts of the country, which makes my work very interesting.

I check today's schedule to make sure I know what will be happening, as well as when and where.

9:00 a.m.   My job involves a lot of paperwork. Today, I have to arrange **accommodations** for everyone going on location next month. I need to find enough beds in a very small town for about fifty people.

11:00 a.m.   I've been given some script changes and have to make sure everyone who needs a copy gets one. I give out as many scripts as I can and make a note of other people who need a copy but are not on the set today.

12:30 p.m.   It's time to check that everyone is in the right costumes and makeup and ready for this afternoon's shoot. I spend a lot of my time checking off names on lists.

Winning an Academy Award is a film director's greatest success.

An assistant director takes care of routine daily tasks so the director won't have to.

1:00 p.m. I watch the shoot and deal with problems and questions that are passed on to me.

5:00 p.m. I'm told about some changes to next week's filming schedule. I quickly type them up and print them out, then rush around giving them to people and putting them on notice boards.

5:30 p.m. The cast and crew are wrapping things up for the day, but I'll be here for a while yet. I need to check that I have done all the tasks on my list for today.

Producer

What is a producer?

Producers have overall responsibility for film, television, radio, or theater productions. While the director is in charge of the creative side of a production, the producer makes sure that the entire project, from the first idea to **promoting** the finished program or show, is a success.

A film or television production has three basic stages, all of which involve the producer:

- preproduction (planning and scheduling)
- production (filming, sound recording, and performing)
- postproduction (editing, marketing, and promoting)

The role of a producer can vary from one production to another, often depending on the type of project. Radio and television producers are usually involved more with creative tasks, while film and theater producers tend to be more concerned with a project's business activities and leave all creative decisions to the directors. Then again, some producers are involved in all aspects of a production, creative and business-related.

Especially in the planning stages of a production, a producer can spend a lot of time making phone calls.

A Production Success Story

The Mousetrap is believed to be the longest continuously running play of any kind in history. This murder mystery by famous crime writer Agatha Christie (1890–1976) started as a thirty-minute radio play called *Three Blind Mice.* The stage version has been playing in London since November 25, 1952.

Producers must sometimes be prepared to take financial risks, even personal ones, because they are often responsible for raising money to finance a production. A film, play, or television project that is successful can make a fortune, but the costs and financial losses of a production that flops can be enormous, creating huge debts for which the producer may be responsible.

Most major film, television, and theater productions are run by large production teams working behind the scenes, while projects such as **documentaries** and game shows often have very small production teams.

Producers will spend some preproduction time trying to "sell" a project to people who can provide financial help.

Main responsibilities of a producer

Preproduction

Producers often have the first idea for a production. The idea can come from a conversation, an event, a book, or a script. Turning a film or theater idea into a production usually requires the following main steps:

- finding financial backing for the project (In some cases, producers are wealthy enough to use their own money. Otherwise, they need support from wealthy people or organizations, or they must convince a financial institution to lend them the money.)
- finding writers to work on the script (Producers often buy the rights to books, then have writers turn them into film or play scripts.)
- finding a director
- selecting actors
- hiring technical staff
- drawing up lists of possible locations for **shooting**

Music often sets the atmosphere of a production so finding exactly the right music is essential.

Good Points and Bad Points

"A career in film can be challenging and exciting, but everybody knows how hard it is to break into the industry, especially for anyone who doesn't have famous contacts or famous parents. All too often, it is who you know, not what you know, that matters most. The important thing is to stay positive and keep developing your skills."

Production

The actual production of a film, theater, or television project can last for anywhere from a few hours to many months, or even years. During this time, a producer's main responsibilities can include:

- making sure that all the different production crews, such as lighting, sound, set construction, and costuming, work well together
- keeping the production on schedule
- monitoring expenses to be sure the production stays within its budget

Postproduction

After a production has been filmed, the producer's jobs can include:

- finding **editors** to create the final version of the film by cutting or keeping different scenes and making sure that the length of the production is within a previously established time frame
- hiring composers to write music for the production and musicians to perform the music
- employing graphic artists to design the on-screen introduction and credits
- marketing and promoting the production, including making sure the film is seen in as many theaters as possible and arranging advance publicity, such as interviews with the production's director or actors

The credits, which are the names seen on-screen at the end of a production, are created by a graphic artist on a computer.

Main qualifications of a producer

Broad production experience
Whether working in films, television, radio, or theater, a producer needs to have a broad range of knowledge, both technical and business-related, about his or her field.

Knowledge of the entertainment market
Producers need to know what kinds of entertainment are currently popular and what kinds of productions are doing well, and they must constantly be keeping up with changes in the entertainment market. Because the popularity of certain types of entertainment can change quickly, timing is extremely important.

Trustworthy and responsible
Producers need to have good reputations and many contacts to get the financial help they need and the best performers and technicians to work for them. Making a film can cost huge amounts of money. **Investors** must know they can trust a producer if they are going to provide financial support.

Producers need to know what the public wants to see.

To find the right people for the production team, a producer often has to do a lot of interviewing.

fact file

Experience and character are the most important requirements to be a producer.

Whatever their education or academic **credentials**, trainees have to prove their worth in practical ways for many years before becoming producers, and no one would consider backing a project without complete trust in the producer.

Persuasive

Producers need to be able to win people's support and be able to convince them that a project will be a success.

Resourceful

At any stage of a production, a lot can go wrong. Investors can suddenly decide to withdraw funding. Work **on location** might run into a long period of bad weather. Leading actors may be injured or become ill. Producers must have the knowledge, skills, and resources to deal with the unexpected, and they must do whatever they can to avoid production delays and to keep production problems from having a bad effect on the cast and crew.

A day in the life of a producer

Shana Gill

Shana has a degree in broadcasting and, for several years, worked part-time producing short films for companies and individuals. She is currently working full-time as the producer of a feature film.

8:00 a.m.   I meet with the director of the film to discuss a possible source of funding that she has found for the project.

We have enough money, right now, to take us through the preproduction and production stages, but I still have to find money for all of the film's postproduction work.

9:30 a.m.   I spend the morning going through my list of contacts, setting up appointments to talk to them about the film and working on a presentation that I hope will persuade them to support the project.

12:00 p.m.   Although I'm still trying to arrange financing, I'm also working on production so I make some phone calls to find filming equipment to rent and **studios** to work in.

In the end, it's the ticket buyers who make a feature film a success.

Producers have to deal with a lot of phone calls and a lot of paperwork.

The days are gone when film companies owned their own studios and equipment. Today, almost everything is rented.

3:30 p.m. I am just about to sit down to work on a progress report when the phone rings. The camera crew that I thought was booked for the production has a problem with the dates I need them. I'll have to set my report aside and get back on the phone.

6:00 p.m. I meet with the director and other key people on the production team to determine when we will be able to actually start filming. Everyone is looking to me for the answers.

Production Designer

What is a production designer?

Production designers, who are also known as **set** designers and scene designers, are responsible for the look, or appearance, of a production, including:

- location, or setting
- background scenery
- set pieces (which include main furnishings and permanent fixtures)
- set decoration
- **props**

A production designer must have a vivid imagination.

Storyboards

Production designers illustrate their creative ideas in a series of sketches, called **storyboards**, to show the progression of a film and its scene and set changes. Storyboards for famous films such as *The Lord of the Rings* and *Titanic* are valuable items for which fans will pay a lot of money.

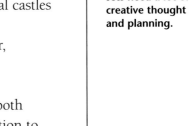

Production design depends on the type of production and might involve any of the following:

- a single set for a television talk show or game show
- several different sets (indoor, outdoor, or both) for a weekly television program
- a spectacular series of sets, such as medieval castles or planets and spaceships, for a film
- a fantasy set, full of color, lights, and glitter, for a pop music video

Even very simple sets need a lot of creative thought and planning.

Production designers are usually involved in both preproduction and production work. In addition to designing sets and props, they often attend filming sessions to see the production in progress and to deal with any problems that come up.

Most production designers are self-employed and work **freelance**, which means that they work under **contract** for a variety of production companies, rather than being employed by one particular company.

Main responsibilities of a production designer

A production designer becomes involved in a production at the very beginning. The preproduction responsibilities usually include:

- reading a script or a production plan or outline to find out what the production is about
- doing background research (For historical productions or foreign settings, designers need to look in libraries and art galleries and on Web sites to find out how people lived in a certain time or place, including the types of homes they had, how they dressed, what they ate, where they worked, and how they spent their free time.)
- meeting with producers and directors to discuss design ideas
- visiting possible sites for a production that will be filmed **on location** to help determine the best choices

The first step in production design is to draw a **technical sketch** of the planned set.

Good Points and Bad Points

"Production design is a cool job, and one that allows you to learn all sorts of different things. You're being paid to learn about something new every day. But the work is also demanding. Very few productions have the luxury of time — even the big ones. You're almost always faced with having to do a lot of work in a short period of time."

After the basic design plans for a production have been decided, the designer has to draw a **floor plan** for each different set that will be needed. Today, most production designers use computers for this part of the work.

It is possible to figure out the cost of building a set from a scale model.

Floor plans are followed by storyboards showing, in sketches, the sequence of scenes and set changes throughout the production. Both the floor plan and storyboard stages usually involve a lot of changes. When the final designs are approved, scale models are built for use by lighting, sound, and costume teams.

As full-size sets are constructed, production designers are responsible for giving instructions to set builders. Production designers for film and television must make sure that sets are suitable for close-up shots, which means paying attention to the smallest details.

Good imagination
Production designers have to be able to come up with ideas for sets that are original, attractive, and add to the success of a production.

Artistic skills and design training
Strong artistic skills are needed to bring design ideas to life, and thorough knowledge of design concepts and techniques are needed to put the ideas in place.

An eye for detail
Audiences are quick to notice anything out of place, from painting flaws to clothing or furniture styles from the wrong time periods, so attention to details is vital.

Business and financial skills
All productions, even very big ones, have budgets. A production designer needs to be as aware as the production's director of how much money can be spent and what the proposed design plans will cost. Production designers must keep expenses within the amounts budgeted for their parts of projects.

Production designers are responsible for supervising set construction.

Computer skills
More and more design work is being done on computers, using **Computer-Aided Design (CAD)** programs and other kinds of art, architectural, and graphic design software.

Every single detail of a set design needs to be checked and rechecked.

fact file

Construction know-how

Because production designers have to supervise set building, they need to understand how sets are constructed. They also need to know a lot about different building materials so they can choose the ones that look the best, wear well, and are the most reasonably priced.

Teamwork

Production design and set construction involve a lot of people. The success of a production depends on all of these people sharing ideas and working well together.

The field of production design attracts people from a variety of backgrounds, including graphic arts, interior design, theater arts, and architecture. In most cases, they have at least a bachelor of arts or bachelor of fine arts degree. Some people enter production design work through film schools or institutes or through programs in theater design or television broadcasting.

A day in the life of a production designer

Gina Lawrence

Gina is a freelance production designer whose projects often involve traveling.

8:30 a.m.   I settle down at my computer, waiting for some ideas to fill my head. I do most of my design plans on a computer so I often work at home. Right now, I'm trying to create set designs for a television series. The series is about a family living in South Africa in the 1950s. Some of the scenes will be shot on location in South Africa, but the indoor scenes will be shot in a **studio**.

I have spent a lot of time studying the history of the time period and looking at photographs, paintings, and anything else that might give me an idea of life and styles in the 1950s.

9:30 a.m.   I get a phone call from a friend who tells me that her aunt lived in South Africa for many years and has loads of photographs and letters. I arrange with my friend to visit her aunt tomorrow.

12:00 p.m.   I attend a meeting with the series' producer, director, and costume designer to discuss production plan details, as well as scheduling.

Production design jobs can involve travel for research or to filming sites.

A production designer's goal is to make the finished set a work of art.

5:00 p.m. The meeting is finally over, and we're exhausted, but we have come up with some good ideas and have set the date for a location visit to South Africa three weeks from now. I have to be prepared for a meeting, a week before we leave, to explain the settings I will be looking for.

6:00 p.m. I'm back at my desk, looking at some more photographs and working on some sketches. My research for a production can go on for a long time, but it has to be done to make sure the finished work looks realistic.

Special Effects Artist

What is a special effects artist?

Special effects artists are the people who create both the realistic and the fantastic scenes and characters seen in films and on television programs. At one time, special effects such as jungle scenes, space aliens, car chases, explosions, volcanoes, and tornadoes were not very realistic and, at times, were so bad they were amusing. It was often very clear to viewers that the trees were made from cardboard, and the walls of houses were so thin that they shook when an actor opened a door.

Today, computer imagery has changed the use of special effects completely, and people often go to see films such as *Star Wars* and *The Lord of the Rings* as much for their fantastic special effects as for their stories.

Computer imagery can produce results that are "out of this world."

Sinking the Titanic

At a cost of about $240 million, the movie *Titanic* is believed to be one of the most expensive films ever made. Special effects included an almost life-size model of the ship, which was built to tilt from side to side. The model was filmed from different angles as it sank in a 17-million-gallon tank of seawater.

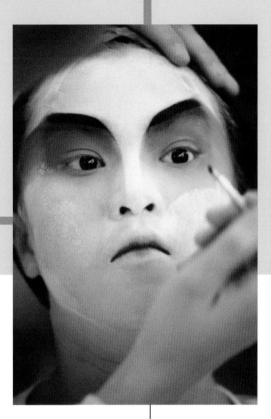

There are two main ways to create special effects:

- physical methods (building a set or a mechnical model, either life-size or scaled down)
- computer methods (creating scenes or action as computer images)

Actors sometimes have to spend many hours with a production's makeup artists.

Another kind of special effect is created by makeup artists. Skilled and clever use of makeup can make a character look older or younger or like someone else entirely. A creative combination of makeup and **prosthetics** can make people look like monsters or other fantastic creatures and make wounds and other kinds of injuries look incredibly real.

Main responsibilities of a special effects artist

The responsibilities of special effects artists depend on the artists' talents or areas of expertise.

- Physical special effects artists build life-size or scale models of cars, ships, buildings, and even entire cities that are correct down to the smallest detail. Then, they blow them up, sink them, set fire to them, or do whatever is needed for the film. Physical special effects called **pyrotechnics** are created by artists who specialize in working with fire and explosives.

- Computer special effects artists usually do their work after a production has been filmed. Computer effects can save production companies a lot of money. They can create scenes that might be impossible or too dangerous to do in real life. They can also alter or improve film shots of real life.

Building scale models takes a lot of time and patience.

Good Points and Bad Points

"I work as a makeup artist on film, television, and theater productions. I'm self-employed and take whatever work comes along, which means I have a variety of different projects. The variety makes my job a lot of fun."

"Some of the work I do can take a very long time, with an actor in makeup for several hours. Being on my feet so long can be tiring."

Some kinds of special effects that are usually best done by computer include taking several shots of a small group of people and combining them to look like a huge crowd; removing unwanted images, such as lamp posts and electrical wires, from scenes; and **enhancing** or improving backgrounds by adding clouds, sunlight, lakes, forests, buildings or other scene-appropriate features.

- Makeup special effects artists use cosmetics, wigs, and prosthetics to improve or change the look of a human body. Latex or foam rubber are used to build big noses and humped backs or to completely change the shape of a person's face. A makeup artist can give an actor a totally different appearance.

Television dramas that show close-up shots of surgical procedures in hospitals rely on makeup special effects artists to create dummy bodies that can be cut open to reveal internal organs. Makeup artists can create very realistic wounds out of rubber and false blood.

Setting up some kinds of special effects calls for a whole team of professionals.

Main qualifications of a special effects artist

Any special effects artist needs to:

- be creative and have a vivid imagination
- enjoy solving problems and finding clever ways of doing things
- have a lot of patience because creating special effects can take a great deal of time

Physical special effects artists need to:

- be very skilled at designing and making models and mechanical objects

Special effects work can be very dangerous.

- be aware of how dangerous their work can be and know how to do it as safely as possible

  Pyrotechnic specialists who work with explosives must be especially careful, and because the use of explosives is regulated by federal, state, and local authorities, they may need special licensing from government agencies to work with them. For added safety, special effects artists using fire in any way may also ask local fire and police departments for assistance.

Makeup artists often use hair pieces and wigs in their work.

Computer special effects artists need to:

- have excellent computer skills
- be able to work with all types of graphics and design programs

Makeup special effects artists need to be:

- skilled in makeup design and application
- knowledgeable about the products and materials they use and their effects on the human body
- friendly, tactful, and able to get along well with all different kinds of people and personalities

fact file

Special effects artists can have almost any kind of education or work experience. What is important are the skills they have developed.

Some physical effects artists have armed forces backgrounds. Others are trained electricians or explosives experts. Computer effects artists have education or training in information technology. Makeup artists often take theatrical makeup courses, then get additional training in special effects.

A day in the life of a special effects artist

Jess Morton

Jess is a **freelance** makeup artist who mainly does special effects work.

8:00 a.m. I gather up my equipment and head off to the **set** of a television commercial. The commercial features two creatures from outer space. I have had meetings with the production team, and I have designs and sketches to work from.

There are two of us working as makeup artists on this project. Luckily, we know each other and get along very well.

8:30 a.m. I set up the makeup area, then make a quick phone call. There's work coming up for a musical, and I want to make sure I'm considered for it.

9:00 a.m. It takes a while to achieve the right look for the space creatures. After we're finished, I will take **digital** photographs of the creatures from several different angles and make notes of what we've done so, if there is a **retake**, the creatures can look exactly the same as they do today.

10:15 a.m. I check for messages on my cell phone and find that the agency recruiting for the musical has left a message and wants me to call back, which, of course, I do immediately.

Great news! I've arranged for an interview next week. I'll have to go through my **portfolio** before the interview to make sure that all the information about my career and the photographs of my work are up to date.

10:30 a.m. The space creatures are ready so I start working on the rest of the cast. Their characters are pretty straightforward and need only a small amount of natural-looking makeup.

11:00 a.m. Filming has started, but I stay to do touch-ups.

5:00 p.m. Filming has ended for today. I'm needed again tomorrow, but if today's shots are good, I won't have to do the space creatures' makeup again.

Computers have become essential tools for creating special effects.

Makeup artists need to know a lot about human faces and forms.

Glossary

accommodations – temporary lodging and related services while traveling

agents – business representatives hired by actors, athletes, authors, and others to negotiate jobs and payment rates

anchors – short for "anchorpersons," who are people who read the news on news broadcasts and introduce reports by other broadcasters

auditions – job interviews for actors, musicians, and other performers, during which candidates demonstrate their skills

bank – a group of similar objects arranged in rows that are one on top of the other

Computer-Aided Design (CAD) – a computer program that helps engineers and architects electronically design anything from airplanes to skyscrapers

contract – a legal agreement that defines a business arrangement between two or more people, exchanging services for a specified amount of money

credentials – documents that verify a person's credits and qualifications

current affairs – newsworthy events that have recently occurred

digital – computerized, using electronic code expressed in individual numbers called digits

documentaries – extended reports for film or television, which deal with factual information that is usually newsworthy

edit – to change or refine in preparation for presentation or publication

enhancing – adding features that improve quality, value, or appearance

floor manager – the person who sets up the studio or stage for a production, takes care of props, and gives instructions to the cast and crew

floor plan – a scale line drawing of the walls, doorways, and window openings of a room or rooms, as seen from above, which may also show the arrangement of furniture in the room or rooms

formats – kinds, or types, based on the choice of material and presentation style

freelance – self-employed and free to work for more than one client

hosting – taking care of the social needs of guests, such as greeting, entertaining, and conversation or information

investors – people who provide money for a production in exchange for a share of the production's profits, or earnings

jibs – the movable, and often motorized, projecting arms of cranes

live – transmitted as it occurs

media – the instruments of mass communication, including newspapers, radio, television, and film

mounts – (n) large platforms or frames that hold heavy objects during use

negotiate – to discuss or deal with another party to arrive at an agreement or settlement of some kind

on location – at the actual place

portfolio – a collection of creative work that demonstrates a person's skills and ability to a potential employer

promoting – working to gain buyers' recognition and acceptance through various kinds of advertising and publicity

props – short for "properties," which are the movable objects used in the action of a production

prosthetics – pieces of latex (rubber), foam, gelatin, and other flexible materials that are attached to actors' faces to change their appearance

pyrotechnics – fiery, explosive displays, such as fireworks, which are often used in film productions as special effects

rehearsal – time spent practicing a performance before it is seen by the public

retake – (n) a new filming session to correct or improve previous filming

rushes – (n) the first prints made of a film after a period of shooting

scenario – a sequence of events or actions

sets – combinations of permanent and movable scenery and furnishings that establish the place, time, and atmosphere for the various scenes of a production

shift – a scheduled period of time when certain groups of workers are on duty

shoot – (v) to film or photograph with a camera; (n) a filming session

storyboards – sequences of drawings depicting the shots that are planned for a filmed production

studio – a room specially equipped for filming, videotaping, or recording sound

taped – (v) recorded, or filmed, on videotape

tech rehearsals – rehearsals at which lighting, sound, and other technical activities are coordinated with the performance of a production

technical sketch – a rough drawing that shows only certain features of a design but also provides information needed by technicians and construction workers

teleprompter – an electronic device that displays a script on a screen that can be seen only by the speakers or performers

trade union – an organization that tries to protect the interests of workers in a particular trade or profession with regard to wages, benefits, and working conditions

tripods – three-legged stands for holding cameras steady while in use

voice-overs – recordings of voices for unseen characters, such as narrators, or film characters whose voices come from behind the scenes

Further Information

This book does not cover all of the jobs that involve working in film and television. Many are not mentioned, including animation, or cartoon, artist; sound engineer; and lighting technician. This book does, however, give you an idea of what working in film and television is like.

The film and television industries attract a great many people so finding a job is not easy. In the exciting world of film and television, people with talent, energy, and determination can do very well. If you want a secure nine-to-five job, however, it probably isn't for you. Many people in film and television work freelance, which means they are self-employed and have to find their own work. Jobs that involve long work hours can be followed by times with very little work or no work at all.

The way to decide if working in film or television is for you is to find out what the work involves. Read about film and television careers and talk to people, especially people you know, who work in the film and television industries.

When you are in middle school or high school, a teacher or career counselor might be able to help you arrange some work experience in a certain career. For careers working in film or television, that experience could mean helping with on-the-air fund-raising for a local public television station or assisting with a community theater production, watching what goes on and how people working there spend their time.

Books

Break a Leg! The Kids' Guide to Acting and Stagecraft
Lise Friedman
(Workman, 2002)

Director: Film, TV, Radio, and Stage
Lewann Sotnak
(Capstone Press, 2000)

Lights, Camera, Action! Making Movies and TV from the Inside Out
Lisa O'Brien
(Maple Tree Press, 1998)

Special Effects in Film and Television
Jake Hamilton
(DK Publishing, 1998)

Web Sites

The Actor's Checklist
www.actorschecklist.com

Career: Camera Operators
www.iseek.org/sv/
13000.jsp?id=100029

Career Browser: Radio and Television Announcers and Newscasters
www.collegeboard.com/
apps/careers/0,1462,4-
088,00.html

Useful Addresses

Actor

Actors' Equity Association
National Headquarters
165 West 46th Street
New York, NY 10036
Tel: (212) 719-9815
www.actorsequity.org

Screen Actors Guild
5757 Wilshire Boulevard
Los Angeles, CA 90036-3600
Tel: (323) 954-1600
www.sag.org

Announcer/Program Host

Broadcast Education Association
1771 N Street, NW
Washington, DC 20036-2891
Tel: (888) 380-7222 or (202) 429-3935
www.beaweb.org

Camera Operator

American Society of Cinematographers
1782 North Orange Drive
Hollywood, CA 90028
Tel: (800) 448-0145
www.theasc.com

Director

Directors Guild of America (DGA)
7920 Sunset Boulevard
Los Angeles, CA 90046
Tel: (800) 421-4173 or (310) 289-2000
www.dga.org

DGA Assistant Director Training Program
East Coast:
   1697 Broadway, Suite 600
   New York, NY 10019
   Tel: (212) 397-0930
   www.dgatrainingprogram.org
West Coast:
   14724 Ventura Boulevard, Suite 775
   Sherman Oaks, CA 91403
   Tel: (818) 386-2545
   www.trainingplan.org

Producer

The Producers Guild of America, Inc.
8530 Wilshire Boulevard, Suite 450
Beverly Hills, CA 90211
Tel: (310) 358-9020
www.producersguild.org/pg/
   about_a/faq.asp

Production Designer

Art Directors Guild
11969 Ventura Boulevard, Suite 2200
Studio City, CA 91604
Tel: (818) 762-9995
www.artdirectors.org/introduction/
   whatis_ad.php

Special Effects Artist

Visual Effects Society
2308 Broadway
Santa Monica, CA 90404
Tel: (310) 315-6055
www.visualeffectssociety.com

Index